TABLE OF CONTENTS

Legal Disclaimer

The information in this book is for educational and informational purposes only. It is not a substitute for professional medical advice, diagnosis, or treatment. Always seek the advice of your physician or qualified health provider with any questions regarding a medical condition. Never disregard professional medical advice or delay seeking it because of something you read in this book.

The author and publisher are not responsible for any adverse effects or consequences resulting from the use of any suggestions, preparations, or procedures discussed. Individual results may vary. Consult with a qualified healthcare professional before starting any new health regimen, especially if you are pregnant, nursing, have a medical condition, or are taking medication.

By reading this book, you acknowledge and agree that the author and publisher are not liable for any loss or damage, including but not limited to special, incidental, consequential, or other damages, that may arise from the use or misuse of the information presented.

Copyright Notice - Hutchinson Publishing 2024

All rights reserved. No part of this book may be reproduced, distributed, or transmitted in any form or by any means without the prior written permission of the publisher, except for brief quotations in reviews and other noncommercial uses permitted by copyright law.

CHAPTER 1: INTRODUCTION

Overview of Witchcraft and Mental Health

Witchcraft has long been a practice that emphasizes the power of nature, the strength of personal intention, and the interconnectedness of all things. In recent years, there has been a growing recognition of how witchcraft can contribute to mental health. This book explores the ways in which the rituals, practices, and philosophies of witchcraft can support mental well-being, providing tools for managing stress, anxiety, depression, and other mental health challenges.

Witchcraft and Wicca offer a unique perspective on mental health, blending traditional healing methods with spiritual practices that foster a deep connection with the natural world. Through the use of herbs, meditation, rituals, and community support, practitioners can create a holistic approach to mental wellness that addresses the mind, body, and spirit.

This book is designed to be a comprehensive guide for anyone looking to integrate witchcraft into their mental health practices. Whether you are a seasoned practitioner or new to the path, you will find valuable insights and practical techniques to enhance your well-being.

The Interconnectedness of Mind, Body, and Spirit

One of the core principles of witchcraft is the belief in the interconnectedness of mind, body, and spirit. This holistic approach recognizes that mental health cannot be viewed in isolation but must be considered in the context of overall well-being.

Mind: The mind is a powerful tool in witchcraft. Thoughts, intentions, and beliefs shape our reality and influence our mental health. Practices like mindfulness, meditation, and visualization help cultivate a positive mental state, reduce anxiety, and improve focus.

Body: The physical body is not only the vessel that carries us through life but also a key component in our mental health. Herbal remedies, nutrition, exercise, and body-based practices such as yoga or tai chi are all integral to maintaining physical and mental balance. When the body is healthy, the mind and spirit are better able to thrive.

Spirit: The spirit connects us to something greater than ourselves, whether that be nature, the universe, or the divine. Spiritual practices in witchcraft, such as rituals, spells, and communion with nature, nourish the soul and provide a sense of purpose and belonging. This spiritual connection can be a powerful source of strength and resilience in the face of mental health challenges.

By addressing the mind, body, and spirit together, witchcraft offers a comprehensive approach to mental health that promotes holistic healing and well-being.

How to Use This Book

This book is structured to provide both theoretical insights and practical tools that you can integrate into your daily life. Each chapter focuses on different aspects of mental health and witchcraft, offering a blend of information, exercises, and rituals to support your journey.

Chapter Overviews:

- Chapter 2: Understanding Mental Health in the Context of Witchcraft: Explores the holistic approaches to mental health within witchcraft, discussing the role of spirituality and common mental health challenges.

- Chapter 3: Herbs and Their Mental Health Benefits: Provides detailed profiles of key herbs, explaining their benefits and how to use them in various remedies.

- Chapter 4: Daily Practices for Mental Health: Offers practical daily rituals and exercises to maintain mental well-being.

- Chapter 5: Rituals and Spells for Mental Well-being: Details specific rituals and spells designed to support mental health.

- Chapter 6: Energy Work and Mental Health: Discusses techniques for balancing chakras, cleansing the aura, and other forms of energy healing.

- Chapter 7: Building a Supportive Community: Highlights the importance of community in mental health, offering ways to create and engage in supportive circles.

- Chapter 8: Advanced Techniques for Mental Health: Introduces more advanced practices such as crafting magical inks, making herb-infused candles, and using talismans.

- Chapter 9: Case Studies and Personal Stories: Shares real-life examples and personal reflections from practitioners who have integrated witchcraft into their mental health practices.

- Chapter 10: Resources and Further Learning: Provides recommendations for further reading, useful websites, and courses to deepen your knowledge.

Using the Book:

- **Read Sequentially or Selectively:** You can read the book from start to finish to gain a comprehensive understanding, or you can jump to specific chapters that address your immediate needs.

- **Practical Exercises:** Throughout the book, you will find practical exercises, rituals, and recipes. Try incorporating these into your routine to see what resonates best with you.

- **Reflection:** Keep a journal to record your experiences, insights, and progress. Reflecting on your journey can provide valuable insights and reinforce your practices.

- **Community Engagement:** Consider sharing your journey with a supportive community. Engaging with others can provide encouragement, new ideas, and a sense of connection.

By weaving the practices and philosophies from this book into your life, you'll find a more balanced and empowered approach to mental health, enriched by the beautiful traditions of witchcraft. Embrace this journey with an open heart and mind, and may it bring you healing, growth, and deep, meaningful connections.

CHAPTER 2: UNDERSTANDING MENTAL HEALTH IN THE CONTEXT OF WITCHCRAFT

Holistic Approaches to Mental Health

Witchcraft, at its core, promotes a holistic approach to mental health, emphasizing the interdependence of the mind, body, and spirit. This comprehensive perspective aligns with many modern holistic health practices, recognizing that mental health cannot be treated in isolation but must be addressed within the context of overall well-being.

Integrating Mind, Body, and Spirit

- **Mind:** Mental health involves maintaining a healthy mindset, emotional balance, and cognitive function. Witchcraft supports mental health through practices such as meditation, affirmations, and visualization, which help cultivate a positive mental state and resilience.

- **Body:** Physical health significantly impacts mental well-being. Herbal remedies, proper nutrition, regular exercise, and sufficient sleep are essential components of this approach. Witchcraft encourages the use of natural remedies and physical practices that support the body's health.

- **Spirit:** Spiritual well-being is a crucial aspect of holistic health. Connecting with the divine, nature, and one's inner self fosters a sense of purpose, belonging, and peace. Rituals, spells, and spiritual practices in witchcraft nurture the spirit, providing a deep sense of fulfillment and connection.

By addressing these three facets of health simultaneously, witchcraft offers a balanced and comprehensive approach to maintaining mental health.

The Role of Spirituality in Mental Well-being

Spirituality plays a vital role in mental well-being, providing a framework for understanding life, finding purpose, and connecting with something greater than oneself. In the context of witchcraft, spirituality is woven into daily practices, rituals, and beliefs, offering numerous benefits for mental health.

Sense of Purpose and Meaning:

Engaging in spiritual practices can give life a greater sense of purpose and meaning. Witchcraft rituals, seasonal celebrations, and personal spiritual practices provide structure and intentionality, which can help combat feelings of aimlessness and depression.

Connection and Community:

Spirituality in witchcraft often involves connecting with nature, deities, and other practitioners. This sense of connection fosters belonging and support, which are crucial for mental health. Participating in group rituals and community gatherings can alleviate loneliness and promote a sense of unity.

Resilience and Coping:

Spiritual practices can enhance resilience and coping mechanisms. The act of performing rituals, casting spells, and setting intentions provides a proactive approach to handling life's challenges. Believing in the efficacy of these practices can empower individuals and improve their ability to cope with stress and adversity.

Mindfulness and Presence:

Many witchcraft practices, such as meditation, grounding, and mindfulness exercises, promote present-moment awareness. These practices reduce anxiety and stress by encouraging individuals to focus on the here and now, rather than worrying about the past or future.

Common Mental Health Challenges and How Witchcraft Can Help

Witchcraft can offer support and tools for managing various common mental health challenges, providing practical and spiritual resources to improve well-being.

Anxiety:

- Grounding Exercises: Techniques such as visualizing roots growing from your feet into the Earth can help alleviate anxiety by promoting a sense of stability and calm.
- Calming Herbs: Herbs like lavender, chamomile, and lemon balm can be used in teas, baths, or as essential oils to reduce anxiety and promote relaxation.
- Protection Spells: Creating protection spells or charms can help individuals feel safer and more secure, reducing anxiety.

Depression:

- Sunlight and Nature: Spending time outdoors and connecting with nature can improve mood and energy levels. Incorporating rituals that honor the sun, like morning sun salutations, can be uplifting.
- Uplifting Herbs: St. John's Wort, lemon balm, and rosemary can help alleviate symptoms of depression. These herbs can be used in teas, tinctures, or aromatherapy.
- Self-Love Rituals: Engaging in rituals that promote self-love and self-care can boost self-esteem and combat feelings of worthlessness. Create a self-love altar with items that inspire joy and positivity.

Stress:

- Mindfulness and Meditation: Regular mindfulness practices and meditation can reduce stress and improve overall mental well-being. Use herbs like peppermint and eucalyptus in your practice to enhance focus and relaxation.

- Cleansing Rituals: Regularly cleansing your space and yourself with smudging or ritual baths can remove negative energy and reduce stress. Use sage, cedar, or lavender for these rituals.

- Energy Healing: Practices like Reiki or chakra balancing can help release stress and restore balance. Use corresponding herbs and essential oils for each chakra to enhance the healing process.

Loneliness:

- Community Involvement: Join or form a coven or spiritual group to foster a sense of belonging and support. Regular gatherings, either in person or online, can provide valuable social connections.
- Rituals of Connection: Perform rituals that connect you with your ancestors, spirit guides, or deities. This can create a sense of spiritual companionship and reduce feelings of isolation.
- Virtual Circles: Engage in virtual witchcraft communities and participate in online rituals and discussions. These connections can be incredibly supportive and enriching.

Burnout:

- Restorative Practices: Incorporate restorative practices such as gentle yoga, meditation, and herbal baths into your routine to combat burnout. Herbs like chamomile, valerian, and lavender can aid in relaxation and recovery.

- Setting Boundaries: Use spells and rituals to set and reinforce personal boundaries. This can help protect your energy and prevent overcommitment.

- Rituals of Renewal: Perform rituals during the new moon to release what no longer serves you and set intentions for renewal and self-care. Use herbs like rosemary and basil for their rejuvenating properties.

By embracing the holistic practices of witchcraft with a focus on mental health, you can create a balanced and supportive approach to your well-being. This chapter lays the groundwork for understanding how witchcraft can be a powerful friend and ally in nurturing and enhancing your mental health.

CHAPTER 3: HERBS AND THEIR MENTAL HEALTH BENEFITS

Overview of Herbal Allies for Mental Health

In the realm of witchcraft, herbs are considered powerful allies that can significantly enhance mental health. These natural gifts from the Earth offer a myriad of benefits, each with its unique properties and applications. The practice of using herbs to support mental well-being is deeply rooted in both historical traditions and modern holistic practices. By integrating these botanical allies into your daily life, you can cultivate a profound sense of balance, calm, and resilience.

Herbs can be used in various forms—teas, tinctures, salves, and essential oils—each offering a different method to harness their healing properties. Whether you seek to alleviate anxiety, combat depression, or simply promote a sense of well-being, there is an herb that can support your journey. This chapter delves into the benefits of key herbs, providing detailed profiles and practical recipes to help you incorporate these powerful plants into your mental health practices.

Detailed Profiles of Key Herbs

Lavender (Lavandula angustifolia)

Lavender is perhaps one of the most beloved herbs in both witchcraft and traditional medicine. Known for its soothing scent and calming properties, lavender is a staple in any herbalist's toolkit. This versatile herb is celebrated for its ability to reduce anxiety, promote relaxation, and improve sleep quality. The gentle, floral aroma of lavender has a profound effect on the nervous system, helping to calm the mind and ease tension.

Lavender can be used in numerous ways: as a tea, essential oil, or even dried and placed in sachets or pillows. Sipping on lavender tea can provide a gentle sedative effect, perfect for winding down before bed. The essential oil, when diffused or applied topically, can alleviate stress and promote a sense of peace. Including lavender in your daily routine can transform your space into a sanctuary of calm and tranquility.

Chamomile (Matricaria chamomilla)

Chamomile is another cornerstone herb in the realm of mental health. Known for its anti-inflammatory and calming properties, chamomile is often used to soothe digestive issues and reduce anxiety. This gentle herb works wonders in promoting relaxation and easing the mind, making it an excellent choice for those struggling with stress or insomnia.

Chamomile tea is a popular remedy for its mild sedative effects, which can help you relax and prepare for a restful night's sleep. Adding chamomile to your bath can also create a soothing experience, helping to calm both the body and mind. This herb's sweet, apple-like aroma is a comforting presence that nurtures a sense of peace and well-being.

St. John's Wort (Hypericum perforatum)

St. John's Wort is renowned for its antidepressant properties and has been used for centuries to lift the spirits and combat mild to moderate depression. This vibrant yellow-flowered herb works by increasing the levels of serotonin, dopamine, and other neurotransmitters in the brain, promoting a more balanced and positive mood.

While St. John's Wort can be incredibly beneficial, it's important to use it with caution, as it can interact with various medications. Always consult with a healthcare provider before incorporating it into your routine. This herb is typically consumed as a tea or tincture, and consistent use over several weeks can lead to noticeable improvements in mood and overall mental well-being.

Lemon Balm (Melissa officinalis)

Lemon balm is cherished for its calming and anti-anxiety properties. With a delightful citrus aroma, this herb has a gentle but effective action on the nervous system, making it an excellent choice for those experiencing stress or restlessness. Lemon balm can help uplift the spirits and promote a sense of calm, making it a perfect addition to your herbal arsenal.

This versatile herb can be enjoyed as a tea, tincture, or infused in oils and baths. Drinking lemon balm tea can provide immediate relief from anxiety and stress, while using it in a bath can create a soothing and relaxing experience. Its bright, refreshing scent also makes it a wonderful herb to grow in your garden or keep in your kitchen.

Peppermint (Mentha × piperita)

Peppermint is widely known for its refreshing and invigorating properties. It acts as a natural stimulant, helping to clear the mind and enhance focus. This herb is particularly useful for combating mental fatigue and promoting a sense of clarity and alertness.

Peppermint tea is a popular choice for its ability to soothe digestive issues and refresh the mind. The essential oil, when diffused or applied topically, can provide an instant burst of energy and focus. Incorporating peppermint into your daily routine can help keep your mind sharp and your spirits lifted.

Creating Herbal Remedies for Mental Health

Integrating herbs into your mental health routine can be a simple and effective way to support overall well-being. Here are some practical methods to harness the healing properties of these botanical allies.

Teas: Creating herbal teas is one of the most accessible and enjoyable ways to benefit from herbs. For example, a calming tea blend might include equal parts of lavender, chamomile, and lemon balm. Steep the herbs in boiling water for about 10 minutes, then strain and enjoy. This tea can be sipped in the evening to promote relaxation and restful sleep.

Tinctures: Tinctures are concentrated herbal extracts that are easy to make and use. To create a tincture, fill a glass jar with fresh or dried herbs, then cover with high-proof alcohol such as vodka. Seal the jar and store it in a cool, dark place for 4-6 weeks, shaking it daily. Strain the liquid into a dropper bottle and label it. A few drops of a St. John's Wort tincture taken daily can help lift the spirits and combat mild depression.

Salves: Herbal salves are healing balms that can be applied to the skin. To make a calming salve, infuse olive oil with chamomile and lavender by placing the herbs in a jar and covering them with oil. Let the mixture sit for several weeks, then strain out the herbs. Melt beeswax in a double boiler, then add the infused oil and stir until combined. Pour the mixture into tins and allow it to cool. This salve can be used to soothe irritated skin and promote relaxation.

Essential Oils: Essential oils capture the concentrated essence of herbs and can be used in a variety of ways. Diffusing lavender or peppermint oil can transform your space into a calming or invigorating environment. You can also create a relaxing massage oil by diluting essential oils in a carrier oil such as almond or jojoba oil. This can be applied to pulse points or used in aromatherapy practices to enhance your mental well-being.

Mix these herbal remedies into your daily routine and you can craft a personalized approach to mental health that nourishes your mind, body, and spirit. Each herb has its own special benefits, and by trying out different preparations, you can discover what suits you best. Embrace the healing power of herbs and let them lead you towards a more balanced and peaceful state of being.

Chapter 4: Daily Practices for Mental Health

Daily Practices for Mental Health

Integrating daily practices into your routine can significantly enhance your mental well-being. These rituals and exercises, rooted in the principles of witchcraft and holistic health, are designed to help you maintain balance, reduce stress, and foster a deep sense of inner peace. By dedicating time each day to these practices, you can create a consistent and nurturing environment for your mental health.

Morning Rituals to Start the Day Right

Starting your day with intention and mindfulness sets a positive tone for the hours ahead. A morning ritual can be a simple yet powerful way to ground yourself, focus your mind, and connect with your inner self.

Morning Meditation: Begin your day with a few minutes of meditation. Find a quiet space where you won't be disturbed. Sit comfortably, close your eyes, and take several deep breaths. Focus on your breathing, allowing any thoughts to pass by without attachment. This practice helps clear the mind and set a peaceful tone for the day.

Sun Salutations: Performing a series of gentle stretches or yoga poses can invigorate the body and mind. Sun salutations are a perfect way to greet the day, combining movement with breath. As you move through each pose, visualize yourself absorbing the sun's energy, filling you with vitality and positivity.

Affirmations: Positive affirmations can shape your mindset and reinforce your intentions for the day. After your meditation or yoga, stand before a mirror and repeat affirmations that resonate with you. Statements like "I am calm and centered," "I am capable and strong," or "I embrace today with an open heart" can boost your confidence and focus.

Evening Practices for Relaxation and Sleep

Just as it's important to start the day with intention, winding down with calming rituals can promote restful sleep and emotional balance. These evening practices can help you release the stresses of the day and prepare for a peaceful night.

Herbal Tea Ritual: A warm cup of herbal tea in the evening can be a comforting way to relax. Choose calming herbs like chamomile, lavender, or lemon balm. As you sip your tea, take a few moments to reflect on your day, acknowledging any accomplishments or challenges. Let go of any lingering tension, and allow the soothing properties of the herbs to calm your mind and body.

Gratitude Journal: Before bed, take a few minutes to write in a gratitude journal. List at least three things you are grateful for that day. This practice shifts your focus from any negative experiences to positive ones, promoting a sense of contentment and peace.

Evening Bath: An herbal bath can be a luxurious way to unwind. Fill a muslin bag with calming herbs like lavender, chamomile, and rose petals, and hang it under the running water as you fill your bath. As you soak, visualize the water washing away any stress or negativity, leaving you refreshed and relaxed.

Mindfulness and Meditation Techniques

Mindfulness and meditation are powerful tools for maintaining mental well-being. These practices help cultivate present-moment awareness, reduce anxiety, and enhance emotional resilience.

Breathing Exercises: Simple breathing exercises can be done anytime, anywhere. One effective technique is the 4-7-8 breath: inhale through your nose for a count of four, hold for a count of seven, and exhale through your mouth for a count of eight. Repeat this cycle several times to calm your mind and body.

Body Scan Meditation: This practice involves paying attention to different parts of your body, noticing any sensations without judgment. Lie down in a comfortable position and close your eyes. Starting from your toes, slowly move your attention up through your body, spending a few moments on each area. This helps you become more aware of physical sensations and promotes relaxation.

Mindful Walking: Take a walk outside, focusing on the sensations of walking. Feel your feet making contact with the ground, notice the movement of your body, and pay attention to the sights, sounds, and smells around you. This practice helps ground you in the present moment and can be especially calming.

Grounding and Centering Exercises

Grounding and centering are essential practices for maintaining emotional stability and balance. These exercises help you stay connected to the Earth and your inner self, providing a sense of stability and calm.

Grounding Visualization: Find a quiet place to sit or stand. Close your eyes and take a few deep breaths. Visualize roots extending from the soles of your feet deep into the Earth. Imagine these roots anchoring you firmly to the ground, drawing up energy and stability. Spend a few minutes visualizing this connection, feeling grounded and centered.

Earthing: Spending time in direct contact with the Earth can be incredibly grounding. Walk barefoot on grass, soil, or sand, and feel the natural energy of the Earth beneath your feet. This simple practice can help you feel more connected and balanced.

Centering Breath: Place one hand on your heart and the other on your abdomen. Take a deep breath in, feeling your abdomen rise, then your chest. Exhale slowly, feeling your chest and then your abdomen fall. Repeat this process several times, focusing on the rhythm of your breath. This exercise helps center your energy and bring you into the present moment.

Blending these daily practices into your routine, you can cultivate a nurturing space for your mental health. Each ritual and exercise is crafted to uplift your mind, body, and spirit, helping you find a deep sense of balance and well-being. Embrace these practices with an open heart, and let them lead you towards a more serene and centered life.

CHAPTER 5: RITUALS AND SPELLS FOR MENTAL WELL-BEING

Protection and Cleansing Rituals

Protection and cleansing rituals are fundamental practices in witchcraft, essential for maintaining a safe and energetically balanced environment. These rituals help clear away negative energies and create a protective barrier around yourself and your space, fostering a sense of security and peace.

Cleansing Ritual: One of the simplest and most effective cleansing rituals involves smudging. Begin by selecting a smudge stick made of sage, cedar, or lavender.

Light the smudge stick and allow it to smolder, producing smoke. Move through your space, wafting the smoke into every corner, while focusing on your intention to cleanse and purify.

As you do this, you might say, "I cleanse this space of all negativity and fill it with light and peace." This ritual not only purifies your environment but also your mind, promoting clarity and tranquility.

Protection Ritual: Creating a protective barrier around your home can provide ongoing security. Start by placing protective herbs such as rosemary, basil, and garlic at the entrances to your home.

You can also create a protection jar by filling a small jar with these herbs, along with a pinch of salt and a protective stone like black tourmaline. Seal the jar with red wax and place it near your front door.

Visualize a protective light surrounding your home, keeping all negativity at bay. This ritual reinforces your personal space as a sanctuary of safety and peace.

Self-Love and Self-Care Spells

Self-love and self-care are crucial for mental well-being, and incorporating witchcraft into these practices can enhance their effectiveness. These spells and rituals nurture your self-esteem and promote emotional healing.

Self-Love Spell: To perform a self-love spell, gather a pink candle, rose petals, and a small piece of rose quartz. Begin by creating a sacred space where you won't be disturbed.

Light the pink candle, symbolizing love and compassion. Scatter the rose petals around the candle, and hold the rose quartz in your hands. Close your eyes and focus on your breath.

Visualize a warm, pink light radiating from your heart, filling you with love and acceptance. Repeat affirmations such as, "I am worthy of love and respect," "I embrace myself fully," and "I am enough."

Allow this energy to fill you completely, and when you're ready, extinguish the candle and carry the rose quartz with you as a reminder of your self-love.

Self-Care Ritual: Create a self-care ritual bath to relax and rejuvenate. Fill your bathtub with warm water and add a handful of Epsom salts, along with a few drops of lavender and chamomile essential oils. You can also add dried rose petals and lavender flowers to the water.

As you soak, focus on releasing any stress or tension, allowing the water to cleanse your body and mind.

Visualize the water absorbing any negativity, and feel yourself becoming lighter and more relaxed. This ritual not only soothes your physical body but also refreshes your spirit, promoting overall well-being.

Healing and Renewal Rituals

Healing and renewal rituals are powerful tools for overcoming emotional wounds and fostering a sense of rebirth. These practices help release past traumas and invite new, positive energies into your life.

Healing Ritual: For a healing ritual, gather a white candle, a piece of amethyst, and healing herbs such as calendula, chamomile, and peppermint.

Begin by lighting the white candle, symbolizing purity and healing. Hold the amethyst in your hands and focus on your intention to heal. You can place the herbs around the candle or create a small sachet to carry with you.

Visualize a bright, healing light surrounding you, washing away pain and hurt.

Say aloud, "I release all that no longer serves me and welcome healing into my life." Allow this light to penetrate every part of your being, bringing peace and renewal. Keep the amethyst close to you to continue the healing process.

Renewal Ritual: To perform a renewal ritual, select a quiet outdoor location, preferably near water. Bring with you a journal, a pen, and a small bowl of water.

Sit comfortably and reflect on the areas of your life where you seek renewal. Write down your thoughts and intentions in your journal. Once you have finished, read them aloud and then tear the pages into small pieces. Place the pieces in the bowl of water, symbolizing the washing away of old energies.

As you do this, say, "I release the old and welcome the new. I am open to growth and transformation." Allow the water to carry away your intentions, and feel a sense of renewal and clarity washing over you.

Using the Moon Phases for Mental Health

The phases of the moon offer a powerful framework for aligning your mental health practices with the natural rhythms of the Earth. Each phase of the moon carries its own unique energy, which can be harnessed to support various aspects of your mental well-being.

New Moon: The new moon is a time of new beginnings and setting intentions. Use this phase to focus on what you want to manifest in your life. Create a vision board or write down your goals and dreams. Perform a ritual where you plant a seed, either literally or symbolically, to represent the new beginnings you are cultivating.

Waxing Moon: As the moon grows, so does its energy. This is a time for building and taking action towards your goals. Focus on practices that support growth and progress. Perform spells for prosperity, health, and personal development. This is also a great time to start new projects or habits that support your mental well-being.

Full Moon: The full moon is a time of culmination and celebration. Use this phase to reflect on your achievements and express gratitude. Perform a full moon ritual by bathing in moonlight, either outside or through a window.

Charge your crystals and tools by placing them under the moonlight. This is also a powerful time for releasing what no longer serves you. Write down anything you wish to let go of and burn the paper, symbolizing release and transformation.

Waning Moon: As the moon decreases in size, it is a time for introspection, release, and rest. Focus on cleansing and banishing negative energies. Perform a cleansing ritual for your home and yourself. Reflect on the past month and identify areas where you need to release and let go. This phase is also an excellent time for deep self-care and rest, allowing your body and mind to rejuvenate.

When embracing these rituals and spells in your practice, you can establish a nurturing and empowering framework for your mental well-being. Each ritual and spell is thoughtfully designed to resonate with the natural rhythms of the Earth and your inner cycles, cultivating a deep sense of balance and harmony. Approach these practices with an open heart, and allow them to lead you towards a more peaceful and empowered way of being.

CHAPTER 6: ENERGY WORK AND MENTAL HEALTH

Understanding the Aura and Chakras

Energy work is a profound aspect of witchcraft and mental health, focusing on the subtle energies that flow through and around us. Central to this understanding are the concepts of the aura and chakras, both of which play crucial roles in our overall well-being.

The Aura: The aura is an electromagnetic field that surrounds every living being, composed of multiple layers that interact with our physical and emotional states. This energetic shield can absorb and emit various energies, reflecting our current mental, emotional, and physical health. A healthy, balanced aura protects us from negative influences and maintains our overall energy equilibrium.

Chakras: Chakras are energy centers within the body that regulate the flow of energy. There are seven main chakras, each associated with specific physical, emotional, and spiritual functions. When these chakras are balanced and aligned, energy flows freely, promoting well-being and mental clarity. However, blockages or imbalances in the chakras can lead to physical ailments, emotional disturbances, and mental health issues.

Using Herbs for Aura Cleansing

Herbs have been used for centuries to cleanse and purify the aura, removing negative energies and restoring balance. Incorporating these practices into your routine can help maintain a healthy and vibrant energy field.

Smudging: One of the most effective methods for cleansing the aura is smudging with sacred herbs. Sage, cedar, and lavender are particularly powerful for this purpose.

To smudge, light the herb bundle and allow it to smolder, producing smoke. Pass the smoke around your body, starting at your feet and moving upwards, while focusing on your intention to cleanse and purify. Visualize the smoke carrying away any negative energies, leaving your aura bright and clear.

Herbal Baths: Taking an herbal bath is another gentle and effective way to cleanse your aura. Fill your bathtub with warm water and add a muslin bag filled with cleansing herbs like rosemary, chamomile, and peppermint.

As you soak, visualize the water absorbing any negativity and refreshing your energy field. This ritual not only cleanses your aura but also promotes relaxation and emotional balance.

Aura Cleansing Spray: Create an aura cleansing spray by combining water, witch hazel, and essential oils of sage, lavender, and rosemary in a spray bottle.

Shake well and spritz around your body whenever you feel the need to clear your energy. This portable method is convenient for use throughout the day, especially in challenging environments.

Chakra Balancing with Herbal Magic

Balancing your chakras with the help of herbs can significantly enhance your mental and emotional health. Each chakra is associated with specific herbs that can be used in various forms to promote harmony and balance.

Root Chakra (Muladhara): The root chakra, located at the base of the spine, is associated with grounding and stability. Herbs like cedar, patchouli, and clove can help balance this chakra. Try using cedarwood essential oil in a diffuser or applying a patchouli-infused oil to your lower back.

Sacral Chakra (Svadhisthana): Located just below the navel, the sacral chakra governs creativity and sexuality. Sandalwood, ylang-ylang, and calendula are beneficial for this chakra. Incorporate these herbs into a bath or use their essential oils during meditation.

Solar Plexus Chakra (Manipura): The solar plexus chakra, located above the navel, is linked to personal power and confidence. Rosemary, chamomile, and lemon balm are excellent for balancing this chakra. Drink a tea made from these herbs or use their essential oils in a massage oil applied to your abdomen.

Heart Chakra (Anahata): The heart chakra, in the center of the chest, is associated with love and compassion. Rose, lavender, and hawthorn can help balance this chakra. Create a heart-opening tea blend or use rose oil in your daily self-care routine.

Throat Chakra (Vishuddha): Located at the throat, this chakra is related to communication and expression. Peppermint, sage, and eucalyptus are ideal for this chakra. Drink peppermint tea or diffuse sage and eucalyptus oils to enhance your communication abilities.

Third Eye Chakra (Ajna): The third eye chakra, located between the eyebrows, governs intuition and insight. Mugwort, juniper, and eyebright are beneficial for this chakra. Use mugwort in a dream pillow or diffuse juniper oil during meditation to enhance your intuitive abilities.

Crown Chakra (Sahasrara): Situated at the top of the head, the crown chakra is connected to spiritual awareness and enlightenment. Lavender, frankincense, and lotus are powerful for this chakra. Incorporate these herbs into your meditation practice or use their oils in a diffuser to promote spiritual connection.

Energy Healing Techniques

Energy healing techniques can profoundly impact your mental health by promoting balance and removing blockages. These practices can be enhanced with the use of herbs, amplifying their healing properties.

Reiki: Reiki is a Japanese energy healing technique that involves the laying on of hands to channel healing energy into the recipient. Incorporating herbs such as lavender and chamomile into a Reiki session can enhance relaxation and promote deeper healing. Place sachets of these herbs near the recipient or use their essential oils in a diffuser.

Crystal Healing: Crystals are powerful tools for balancing and enhancing energy. Combining them with herbs can create a synergistic effect. For example, pairing rose quartz with rose petals can amplify the healing energy of the heart chakra. Create a crystal grid incorporating both crystals and herbs to focus healing energy on specific areas.

Chakra Meditation: Meditation focused on the chakras can help balance and align your energy centers. Incorporate herbs associated with each chakra into your meditation practice. Burn incense or diffuse essential oils that correspond to the chakra you are focusing on to deepen the meditative experience.

Herbal Energy Baths: Energy baths using specific herbs can help cleanse and rejuvenate your energy field. Combine herbs like rosemary, chamomile, and lavender in a muslin bag and place it in your bathwater. As you soak, visualize the herbs infusing your body with healing energy, balancing your chakras, and cleansing your aura.

By getting to know your aura and chakras and blending herbs into these practices, you can build a powerful system to support your mental and emotional health. Approach these techniques with intention and an open heart, letting the natural energies of herbs and your own inner strength lead you towards greater balance and well-being.

CHAPTER 7: BUILDING A SUPPORTIVE COMMUNITY

The Importance of Community in Mental Health

Community plays a vital role in mental health, providing support, connection, and a sense of belonging. In the context of witchcraft, community offers a space where individuals can share their experiences, learn from one another, and perform rituals together, fostering collective healing and growth.

Being part of a community helps combat loneliness, reduces stress, and enhances overall well-being. It is in these circles that we find validation, encouragement, and the strength to overcome challenges.

Engaging with others who share similar beliefs and practices can be incredibly enriching. The sense of kinship and mutual understanding that develops within a witchcraft community creates a strong foundation for mental health.

Knowing that you are not alone in your spiritual journey can provide comfort and empowerment, making the path of personal and spiritual growth less daunting.

Creating and Leading Sacred Circles

Creating a sacred circle is a profound way to build community and offer support to others. A sacred circle is a group of individuals who come together regularly to practice witchcraft, share knowledge, and support one another. These gatherings can be as formal or informal as desired, depending on the needs and preferences of the group.

Starting a Sacred Circle: To start a sacred circle, begin by identifying individuals who share your interest in witchcraft and mental health. This could be friends, family, or members of your local or online community. Once you have a group, decide on a regular meeting time and place. It's important to create a safe and welcoming environment where everyone feels comfortable sharing and participating.

Setting Intentions: Before each gathering, set clear intentions for the circle. This could be focusing on a specific theme, such as healing, protection, or empowerment. Setting intentions helps to guide the energy of the group and ensures that everyone is working towards a common goal.

Creating Rituals: Incorporate rituals into your gatherings that foster connection and healing. Begin each meeting with a grounding exercise or meditation to center the group. Follow with a sharing circle where each member can speak about their experiences, challenges, and successes. Conclude with a collective ritual or spell that aligns with the group's intentions. This could be a group healing spell, a protection charm, or a ritual to honor the full moon.

Leading with Compassion: As a leader, it's important to approach each gathering with compassion and openness. Encourage participation, but also respect each member's comfort level. Foster an environment of mutual respect and support, where everyone's voice is heard and valued.

Community Healing Rituals

Community healing rituals are powerful tools for collective well-being. These rituals harness the combined energy of the group to promote healing, protection, and empowerment for all members. Here are some ideas for community healing rituals that can be incorporated into your sacred circle.

Group Healing Circle: A group healing circle focuses on collective healing and support. Begin by forming a circle and holding hands. Light a candle in the center to symbolize the group's collective energy. Each member takes turns speaking their intention for healing, whether it be for themselves, another member, or the wider community. As each person speaks, the group focuses their energy on that intention, visualizing healing light surrounding the individual or situation.

Protection Ritual: Create a protection ritual to shield the group from negativity and harm. Gather protective herbs such as sage, rosemary, and garlic. Form a circle and pass the herbs around, allowing each member to hold and infuse them with their protective energy. Once everyone has had a turn, place the herbs in a central bowl and light a candle. As the candle burns, visualize a protective barrier forming around the group, keeping all negativity at bay.

Full Moon Ritual: Harness the energy of the full moon for a community empowerment ritual. Gather outside under the moonlight or create a moonlit space indoors. Begin with a grounding exercise, then form a circle and hold hands.

Each member takes turns speaking their intention for empowerment and growth. As each person speaks, the group visualizes the moon's light infusing them with strength and courage. Conclude with a collective chant or song to raise the energy and solidify the intentions.

Sharing Knowledge and Experiences

Sharing knowledge and experiences within the community is essential for collective growth and learning. Each member brings unique insights and wisdom that can benefit the group as a whole.

Workshops and Classes: Organize workshops and classes where members can share their expertise on various aspects of witchcraft and mental health. This could include herbalism, divination, energy work, or ritual crafting. These sessions provide valuable learning opportunities and foster a sense of collaboration and support.

Story Circles: Create opportunities for members to share their personal stories and experiences. Story circles are a powerful way to build empathy and understanding within the group. Each member takes turns sharing a personal story, while the rest of the group listens with open hearts and minds. This practice strengthens bonds and provides a platform for mutual support and encouragement.

Resource Sharing: Encourage members to share resources such as books, websites, and articles that they have found helpful. Create a communal library or online resource list where members can access and contribute valuable information. This collective pool of knowledge enhances the group's learning and growth.

Mentorship: Establish a mentorship program where more experienced practitioners can guide and support newer members. Mentorship provides personalized support and fosters a deeper sense of connection and community. Mentors can offer guidance, answer questions, and provide encouragement as newer members navigate their spiritual journeys.

Building a supportive community within the framework of witchcraft not only enhances individual mental health but also creates a powerful network of mutual support and growth.

By creating and leading sacred circles, participating in community healing rituals, and sharing knowledge and experiences, you can foster a nurturing and empowering environment for yourself and others. Embrace the power of community, and let it strengthen and uplift you on your journey.

CHAPTER 8: ADVANCED TECHNIQUES FOR MENTAL HEALTH

Crafting Herbal Inks and Dyes for Mental Health Practices

Crafting herbal inks and dyes is a unique and creative way to incorporate the healing properties of herbs into your mental health practices. These inks and dyes can be used for writing affirmations, drawing sigils, or creating art that embodies your intentions and desires. By infusing your creative expressions with the power of herbs, you can amplify your mental and emotional well-being.

Herbal Inks: To create herbal ink, you will need dried herbs, water, and a binding agent such as gum arabic. Choose herbs that align with your mental health goals. For example, lavender for calm, rosemary for clarity, or chamomile for peace.

1. Start by boiling a handful of your chosen herbs in a small pot of water. Let it simmer until the water reduces by half and becomes a deep, concentrated color.
2. Strain the liquid to remove the plant material, then return the liquid to the pot.
3. Add a small amount of gum arabic to the liquid and stir until it dissolves. This will thicken the ink and help it adhere to paper.
4. Allow the ink to cool, then transfer it to a small bottle with a tight lid for storage.

Use your herbal ink for writing affirmations, drawing protective sigils, or creating meaningful art. Each time you use the ink, you are connecting with the energy and properties of the herbs, reinforcing your intentions and promoting mental clarity.

Herbal Dyes: Herbal dyes can be used to color fabrics, papers, or other materials that you use in your mental health practices. To make an herbal dye, follow a similar process to making ink, but without the binding agent.

1. Choose herbs that correspond to your desired outcome. For example, use mint for invigoration, sage for purification, or hibiscus for love.
2. Boil the herbs in water until you achieve a rich, deep color.
3. Strain the liquid to remove the herbs, then transfer the dye to a large container.
4. Soak your chosen material in the dye until it reaches the desired color. This could be fabric for an altar cloth, paper for journal pages, or any other material that holds personal significance.

Using these dyed materials in your rituals and practices adds an extra layer of intention and energy, enhancing your mental health and spiritual work.

Making Herb-Infused Candles for Mental Clarity and Focus

Herb-infused candles are a powerful tool for enhancing mental clarity, focus, and emotional balance. These candles combine the therapeutic benefits of aromatherapy with the illuminating power of fire, creating a multi-sensory experience that supports your mental health.

Materials Needed:

- Beeswax or soy wax
- Essential oils of herbs such as rosemary, peppermint, or eucalyptus
- Dried herbs corresponding to your intentions
- Candle wicks
- Candle molds or containers
- Double boiler for melting wax

Instructions:

1. Begin by melting the wax in a double boiler. As the wax melts, focus on your intention for the candle. Visualize the energy of clarity, focus, or peace infusing the wax.
2. Once the wax is melted, add a few drops of essential oils. Rosemary oil is excellent for mental clarity and focus, while lavender oil can help calm and center the mind.
3. Stir in dried herbs that correspond to your intention. For example, add dried rosemary for clarity, peppermint for invigoration, or chamomile for relaxation.
4. Place the candle wick in the center of your mold or container, then carefully pour the infused wax around it.
5. Allow the candle to cool and solidify completely before trimming the wick.

Light your herb-infused candle during meditation, study sessions, or any time you need to enhance your mental focus and clarity. As the candle burns, it releases the beneficial properties of the herbs, creating a supportive and healing environment.

Using Talismans and Amulets for Ongoing Support

Talismans and amulets have been used for centuries to provide ongoing support, protection, and empowerment. These objects, imbued with specific intentions and energies, can be carried with you or placed in your environment to continuously reinforce your mental and emotional well-being.

Creating a Talisman: A talisman is an object created with the intention of bringing good fortune, protection, or specific energies into your life. To create a talisman for mental health:

1. Choose an object that holds personal significance, such as a piece of jewelry, a stone, or a small pouch.
2. Select herbs that correspond to your desired outcome. For example, carry lavender for calm, basil for protection, or rose petals for self-love.
3. Infuse the object with your intention by holding it in your hands and focusing on your desired outcome. Visualize the energy of the herbs and your intention merging with the object.
4. You can further enhance the talisman by anointing it with essential oils or inscribing it with symbols or sigils that represent your intention.

Carry your talisman with you, or place it in a significant location, such as your altar or bedside table. Each time you see or touch the talisman, it will reinforce your intention and provide ongoing support.

Creating an Amulet: An amulet is typically worn to provide protection and support. To create an amulet for mental health:

1. Choose a piece of jewelry, such as a pendant or bracelet, that you can wear regularly.
2. Select a small charm or stone that corresponds to your intention. For mental clarity, you might choose clear quartz; for emotional balance, amethyst; for grounding, hematite.
3. Infuse the charm with your intention by holding it and visualizing your desired outcome. Focus on the energy you wish to bring into your life, such as clarity, calm, or protection.
4. Attach the charm to your jewelry, and wear it as a reminder of your intention.

Wearing an amulet keeps your intention close to you, providing continuous reinforcement and support throughout your day.

Adopting these advanced techniques into your mental health routine, you'll deepen your bond with the healing properties of herbs and the strength of your own intentions.

Crafting herbal inks and dyes, making herb-infused candles, and using talismans and amulets are wonderful ways to boost your mental clarity, focus, and overall well-being.

Embrace these practices with creativity and purpose, and let them guide and support you on your journey to mental and emotional harmony.

CHAPTER 9: CASE STUDIES AND PERSONAL STORIES

Real-Life Examples of Witchcraft Supporting Mental Health

Incorporating witchcraft into mental health practices has transformed the lives of many individuals, providing them with unique tools for healing and personal growth. Here are a few real-life examples of how witchcraft has supported mental health.

Sarah's Journey to Overcome Anxiety: Sarah, a 34-year-old graphic designer, struggled with severe anxiety for most of her adult life. Traditional therapy and medication provided some relief, but she still felt overwhelmed.

Sarah turned to witchcraft, initially drawn by its emphasis on nature and the cycles of the moon. She began incorporating grounding exercises and herbal teas into her daily routine. Lavender and chamomile tea became a nightly ritual, helping her to unwind and sleep better.

Sarah also created a protection charm that she carried with her, which gave her a tangible sense of security. Over time, these practices helped reduce her anxiety, providing a holistic complement to her traditional treatments.

Mark's Battle with Depression: Mark, a 45-year-old teacher, faced a long battle with depression after a series of personal losses. Feeling disconnected and hopeless, he sought solace in nature and spiritual practices.

Mark found witchcraft through a friend and began practicing daily meditation and visualization techniques. He created a sacred space in his home where he performed rituals focused on healing and renewal.

Herbs like rosemary and lemon balm played a crucial role in his recovery, with Mark using them in baths and teas. The act of performing rituals and connecting with nature provided Mark with a renewed sense of purpose and slowly helped lift the fog of depression.

Lisa's Path to Self-Love: Lisa, a 28-year-old writer, struggled with self-esteem issues and a negative self-image. She discovered witchcraft and its focus on self-love and empowerment.

Lisa began incorporating self-love spells and rituals into her life. She crafted a self-love altar with rose quartz, pink candles, and rose petals, and performed rituals that included affirmations and meditations.

Over time, these practices helped Lisa cultivate a more positive self-image and a deeper sense of self-worth.

Interviews with Practitioners

To gain deeper insights into how witchcraft supports mental health, we conducted interviews with several experienced practitioners who have successfully integrated these practices into their lives.

Interview with Julia, a Herbalist and Witch

Q: How did you first come to combine herbalism and witchcraft in your mental health practices?

A: "I've always been drawn to both herbalism and witchcraft. For me, they naturally complement each other. When I started experiencing anxiety and stress, I turned to herbs for relief. Over time, I realized that incorporating rituals and intentions into my herbal practices made them even more effective. Creating herbal teas with specific intentions, like calming the mind or promoting sleep, added a layer of magic that significantly enhanced my mental well-being."

Q: Can you share a specific ritual that has been particularly effective for you?

A: "One of my favorite rituals is a moonlight herbal bath. I combine lavender, chamomile, and rose petals in a muslin bag and let it infuse in my bathwater under the full moon. I focus on releasing negativity and inviting peace into my life. This ritual has become a monthly practice that deeply rejuvenates my mind and spirit."

Interview with David, a Coven Leader

Q: How has leading a coven impacted your mental health and that of your members?

A: "Leading a coven has been incredibly fulfilling. It creates a strong sense of community and support. We share our experiences, perform group rituals, and support each other through challenges. This sense of belonging and mutual support has been a significant mental health boost for all of us. We perform collective healing rituals that are particularly powerful, harnessing the combined energy of the group."

Q: What advice would you give to someone new to witchcraft looking to improve their mental health?

A: "Start with simple practices and build from there. Grounding exercises, herbal teas, and basic protection spells are great starting points. Don't be afraid to reach out and connect with others. Community is a powerful aspect of witchcraft that can provide much-needed support and encouragement."

Personal Reflections and Lessons Learned

Emily's Reflection on Transformation

:Emily, a 38-year-old artist, reflects on how witchcraft transformed her approach to mental health. "When I first started practicing witchcraft, I was in a dark place. Anxiety and depression seemed insurmountable. But through daily rituals, herbal practices, and connecting with a supportive community, I found a path to healing. Witchcraft taught me the importance of intention and mindfulness. Every spell and ritual became a way to reclaim my power and center myself. The process was gradual, but each step brought me closer to balance and peace. The biggest lesson I learned is that healing is a journey, and it's okay to take it one step at a time."

Alex's Journey of Self-Discovery

Alex, a 25-year-old student, shares his journey of self-discovery through witchcraft. "Witchcraft helped me connect with my inner self in ways I never thought possible. Through meditation, journaling, and working with crystals and herbs, I uncovered parts of myself that I had long ignored. The rituals became a form of therapy, allowing me to process emotions and experiences in a safe, sacred space. One of the most profound experiences was creating a vision board during a new moon ritual. It helped me visualize my goals and align my actions with my intentions."

Sophia's Experience with Community Healing

Sophia, a 30-year-old therapist, reflects on the power of community healing in her practice. "As a therapist, I always understood the importance of community, but it wasn't until I joined a coven that I truly experienced it. The sense of belonging and mutual support was transformative. We performed rituals together, shared our struggles and triumphs, and celebrated the cycles of nature. The collective energy of the group amplified our individual healing processes. Leading group meditations and healing circles became a cornerstone of my practice, both professionally and personally. The lesson I take away is that we heal better together."

These personal stories and reflections highlight the profound impact that witchcraft can have on mental health. Through real-life examples, interviews with practitioners, and personal reflections, this chapter illustrates the diverse ways in which witchcraft supports and enhances mental well-being. Embrace these stories as inspiration and guidance on your own journey towards mental and emotional balance.

CHAPTER 10: SCIENTIFIC BACKING FOR WITCHCRAFT PRACTICES IN MENTAL HEALTH

Integrate Scientific Studies

To provide a stronger foundation for the practices detailed in this book, it's crucial to incorporate scientific research supporting the use of herbs, meditation, and other holistic practices. This approach not only validates the efficacy of these practices but also appeals to a wider audience, including those who may be sceptical of witchcraft. Below are several key areas where scientific studies can be integrated:

Herbal Medicine

Lavender: Numerous studies have shown that lavender can significantly reduce anxiety levels. A study published in the *Journal of Clinical Psychopharmacology* found that Silexan, an oral lavender oil preparation, was as effective as lorazepam (a commonly prescribed anti-anxiety medication) in reducing anxiety symptoms. This indicates that lavender could be a valuable alternative or complementary treatment for anxiety disorders.

Chamomile: Research published in *Phytomedicine* demonstrated that chamomile extract can significantly reduce symptoms of generalized anxiety disorder (GAD), suggesting its potential as a therapeutic agent for anxiety. This supports the inclusion of chamomile in mental health practices, particularly for its calming and sedative effects.

St. John's Wort: Several clinical trials have shown that St. John's Wort is effective in treating mild to moderate depression. A meta-analysis in the *British Medical Journal* concluded that St. John's Wort was superior to placebo and as effective as standard antidepressants, with fewer side effects. This makes it a viable option for those seeking natural remedies for depression.

Meditation and Mindfulness

Mindfulness Meditation: A systematic review and meta-analysis published in *JAMA Internal Medicine* found that mindfulness meditation programs can improve anxiety, depression, and pain, highlighting the effectiveness of these practices in managing mental health conditions. Incorporating mindfulness meditation into daily routines can significantly enhance emotional resilience and reduce stress.

Transcendental Meditation: Research in the *Journal of Alternative and Complementary Medicine* indicated that transcendental meditation can significantly reduce stress and promote emotional stability. This practice provides a valuable tool for those looking to manage their mental health through meditative techniques.

Holistic Practices

Yoga: Studies have shown that yoga can be an effective complementary therapy for mental health conditions. Research published in the *Journal of Psychiatric Practice* found that yoga can reduce symptoms of depression and anxiety, improve mood, and enhance overall well-being. Regular yoga practice can thus be a powerful addition to mental health routines.

Tai Chi: A review in the *American Journal of Health Promotion* concluded that Tai Chi can improve mood and quality of life, reduce stress, and enhance psychological well-being. This makes Tai Chi a beneficial practice for maintaining mental and emotional balance.

Expert Interviews

To further validate the practices and provide a professional perspective on the benefits of integrating witchcraft with mental health, conducting interviews with psychologists, herbalists, and other experts offers valuable insights. Below are highlights from several expert interviews:

Interview with a Psychologist

Dr. Janice Robertson, Clinical Psychologist

Q: How do you see the integration of holistic practices such as meditation and herbal remedies in mainstream mental health treatment?

A: "There is a growing body of evidence supporting the effectiveness of holistic practices. Integrating these into mainstream mental health treatment can provide patients with additional tools for managing stress, anxiety, and depression. Practices like mindfulness meditation are already widely accepted and recommended by many mental health professionals."

Interview with a Herbalist

Emily Mortimer, Certified Herbalist

Q: What are the most effective herbs for managing anxiety and how do they work?

A: "Herbs like lavender, chamomile, and valerian root are highly effective for managing anxiety. They work by interacting with neurotransmitters in the brain, promoting relaxation and reducing stress. Lavender, for example, has been shown to modulate the activity of the parasympathetic nervous system, helping to calm the body and mind."

Interview with a Naturopathic Doctor

Dr. Alan Martin, Naturopathic Doctor

Q: Can you explain the role of holistic practices in mental health from a naturopathic perspective?

A: "Holistic practices play a crucial role in mental health from a naturopathic standpoint. We believe in treating the whole person—mind, body, and spirit. Techniques such as yoga, Tai Chi, and herbal medicine not only address the symptoms but also target the underlying causes of mental health issues, promoting overall balance and well-being."

Chapter 11: Additional Rituals and Practices

Seasonal Practices

Seasonal practices are deeply rooted in the cycles of nature, reflecting the changes in the environment and our inner selves. By aligning our rituals with the seasons, we can harness the natural energies to support our mental health and well-being.

Spring (March 20 - June 20)

- Focus: Renewal and growth.
- Practices: Engage in rituals that promote new beginnings and personal growth. Planting seeds, both literally and metaphorically, can symbolize new projects or goals. Create an altar with symbols of spring such as fresh flowers, green candles, and crystals like green aventurine for growth and prosperity.

Summer (June 21 - September 21)

- Focus: Abundance and vitality.
- Practices: Celebrate the peak of light and energy with rituals that enhance vitality and joy. Spend time outdoors, absorb the sun's energy, and perform rituals to boost your confidence and self-expression. Use sunflowers, citrine, and bright yellow candles in your rituals to symbolize the vibrant energy of summer.

Autumn (September 22 - December 20)

- Focus: Harvest and reflection.
- Practices: This is a time to reflect on your achievements and prepare for the coming winter. Perform rituals that focus on gratitude and letting go of what no longer serves you. Incorporate autumnal elements like leaves, pumpkins, and stones like carnelian to ground your energy and bring a sense of closure.

Winter (December 21 - March 19)

- Focus: Rest and introspection.
- Practices: Use this season to go inward and focus on self-care and healing. Engage in meditative practices, journaling, and rituals that promote peace and introspection. Use winter greens, pine cones, and crystals like amethyst to enhance your practices.

Lunar Practices

Working with lunar phases allows us to tap into the moon's energy, aligning our rituals with its cycles for maximum impact on our mental well-being.

New Moon

- Focus: New beginnings and setting intentions.
- Practices: Use this phase to set goals and intentions. Create vision boards or write down your aspirations. Light a white candle to symbolize new beginnings and meditate on your desires.

Waxing Moon

- Focus: Growth and manifestation.
- Practices: Perform rituals that support the growth of your intentions. Engage in activities that build towards your goals, and use green candles and herbs like basil and rosemary to boost your efforts.

Full Moon

- Focus: Culmination and celebration.
- Practices: Reflect on your achievements and express gratitude. Perform full moon rituals like charging crystals, moon baths, and releasing ceremonies. Use silver or blue candles and moonstone to enhance the lunar energy.

Waning Moon

- Focus: Letting go and banishment.
- Practices: Use this phase to release negativity and cleanse your space. Perform banishing rituals, smudging, and decluttering. Use black candles and herbs like sage and eucalyptus for purification.

Advanced Techniques

For those looking to deepen their practice, here are some advanced techniques that can take your mental and spiritual work to the next level.

Astral Projection

Astral projection involves consciously separating your astral body from your physical body to explore other dimensions and realms. This practice can offer profound insights and healing.

- Preparation: Ensure you are in a safe, quiet space. Meditate to calm your mind and body.
- Technique: Lie down and relax completely. Visualize yourself rising out of your body and floating upwards. Focus on moving through different spaces, and allow your astral body to guide you.
- Returning: Always set the intention to return safely to your body. Gently guide yourself back, and take time to ground yourself afterwards.

Deeper Energy Work

Deep energy work involves advanced practices to cleanse, balance, and enhance your energy field. This can include working with chakras, auras, and meridian lines.

- Chakra Balancing: Use crystals and meditation to focus on each chakra. Visualize each chakra spinning and glowing brightly. Use specific crystals like red jasper for the root chakra, citrine for the solar plexus, and lapis lazuli for the third eye.
- Aura Cleansing: Perform regular aura cleanses using smudging, salt baths, and energy brushes. Visualize a bright light cleansing your aura, removing any negative attachments.

Complex Spell Crafting

Complex spell crafting involves creating multi-step spells that combine various elements like herbs, crystals, candles, and incantations.

- Design Your Spell: Clearly define your intention. Choose elements that correspond to your goal (e.g., herbs, crystals, colours).
- Ritual Setup: Set up your altar with all necessary components. Create a sacred space using circle casting and calling the quarters.
- Spell Casting: Perform each step with focused intention. For example, you might start with a cleansing, then move to an invocation, followed by the main spell work, and end with a grounding and closing.
- Follow-Up: Monitor the results of your spell and make notes in your journal. Reflect on the effectiveness and any adjustments needed for future spells.

Chakra System

The chakra system consists of seven main energy centers in the body, each associated with specific physical, emotional, and spiritual functions. The following list provides a concise overview of each chakra, including its location, associated color, key functions, and balancing herbs and crystals.

Chakra System Overview

Root Chakra (Muladhara)

- Location: Base of the spine
- Color: Red
- Key Functions: Grounding, stability, survival
- Balancing Herbs: Cedar, Patchouli, Clove
- Crystals: Red Jasper, Hematite

Sacral Chakra (Svadhisthana)

- Location: Below the navel
- Color: Orange
- Key Functions: Creativity, sexuality, pleasure
- Balancing Herbs: Sandalwood, Ylang-Ylang, Calendula
- Crystals: Carnelian, Orange Calcite

Solar Plexus Chakra (Manipura)

- Location: Above the navel
- Color: Yellow
- Key Functions: Personal power, confidence, self-esteem
- Balancing Herbs: Rosemary, Chamomile, Lemon Balm
- Crystals: Citrine, Tiger's Eye

Heart Chakra (Anahata)

- Location: Center of the chest
- Color: Green
- Key Functions: Love, compassion, emotional balance
- Balancing Herbs: Rose, Lavender, Hawthorn
- Crystals: Rose Quartz, Green Aventurine

Throat Chakra (Vishuddha)

- Location: Throat
- Color: Blue
- Key Functions: Communication, self-expression, truth
- Balancing Herbs: Peppermint, Sage, Eucalyptus
- Crystals: Lapis Lazuli, Aquamarine

Third Eye Chakra (Ajna)

- Location: Between the eyebrows
- Color: Indigo
- Key Functions: Intuition, insight, psychic abilities
- Balancing Herbs: Mugwort, Juniper, Eyebright
- Crystals: Amethyst, Sodalite

Crown Chakra (Sahasrara)

- Location: Top of the head
- Color: Violet
- Key Functions: Spirituality, enlightenment, connection to the divine
- Balancing Herbs: Lavender, Frankincense, Lotus
- Crystals: Clear Quartz, Amethyst

Phases of the Moon and Their Influences

New Moon

- Focus: New beginnings, setting intentions
- Activities: Vision boards, goal setting, planting seeds (literal and metaphorical)

Waxing Crescent

- Focus: Growth, development
- Activities: Taking action towards goals, nurturing intentions

First Quarter

- Focus: Challenges, decisions
- Activities: Overcoming obstacles, adjusting plans

Waxing Gibbous

- Focus: Refinement, patience
- Activities: Fine-tuning efforts, preparing for completion

Full Moon

- Focus: Culmination, celebration
- Activities: Reflecting on achievements, expressing gratitude, releasing ceremonies

Waning Gibbous

- Focus: Introspection, gratitude
- Activities: Reflecting, giving thanks, sharing knowledge

Last Quarter

- Focus: Release, transition
- Activities: Letting go of what no longer serves, decluttering

Waning Crescent

- Focus: Rest, renewal
- Activities: Resting, rejuvenating, preparing for new beginnings

Properties of Common Herbs

Lavender

- Key Properties: Calming, reduces anxiety, promotes sleep
- Uses: Teas, essential oils, sachets, baths

Chamomile

- Key Properties: Anti-inflammatory, reduces anxiety, promotes relaxation
- Uses: Teas, baths, aromatherapy

St. John's Wort

- Key Properties: Antidepressant, mood-lifting
- Uses: Teas, tinctures (with caution)

Lemon Balm

- Key Properties: Anti-anxiety, uplifting, digestive aid
- Uses: Teas, tinctures, baths

Peppermint

- Key Properties: Refreshing, invigorating, clears the mind
- Uses: Teas, essential oils, topical application

Rosemary

- Key Properties: Enhances memory, stimulates circulation
- Uses: Teas, essential oils, culinary uses

Sage

- Key Properties: Cleansing, purifying, protective
- Uses: Smudging, teas, essential oils

Eucalyptus

- Key Properties: Decongestant, antibacterial, stimulating
- Uses: Essential oils, teas, baths

Expand your rituals to include seasonal and lunar practices and introducing advanced techniques, you can create a richer, more effective approach to mental health and spiritual well-being. These practices provide deeper connections with nature, the cosmos, and your inner self, enhancing your journey towards balance and empowerment.

CHAPTER 12: RESOURCES AND FURTHER LEARNING

Recommended Books and Articles

Expanding your knowledge through reading is an excellent way to deepen your understanding of witchcraft and its applications for mental health. Here are some highly recommended books and articles that offer valuable insights, practical advice, and inspiration.

Books:

- "The Green Witch's Encyclopedia: Herbs, Magic & Healing by Mark Hutchinson: This comprehensive guide offers a treasure trove of knowledge for both novice and experienced practitioners. Explore the ancient wisdom of plants, their healing properties, and their magical correspondences.

- "Cunningham's Encyclopedia of Magical Herbs" by Scott Cunningham: A detailed reference book on the magical properties of herbs, perfect for anyone looking to integrate herbal magic into their mental health practices.

- "The Complete Book of Incense, Oils & Brews" by Scott Cunningham: This book offers recipes and instructions for creating magical brews, incense, and oils that can support mental and emotional well-being.

- "The Witch's Book of Self-Care: Magical Ways to Pamper, Soothe, and Care for Your Body and Spirit" by Arin Murphy-Hiscock: Focuses on self-care practices, including rituals and spells designed to promote mental health and well-being.

- "Psychic Witch: A Metaphysical Guide to Meditation, Magick & Manifestation" by Mat Auryn: Provides techniques for enhancing your psychic abilities, meditations, and magical practices that support mental clarity and emotional balance.

- "The Crystal Bible" by Judy Hall: A comprehensive guide to crystals and their healing properties, useful for anyone interested in incorporating crystals into their mental health practices.

Articles:

- "The Healing Power of Herbs" by Dr. Tieraona Low Dog: This article explores the science behind the healing properties of herbs and their applications for mental health.
- "Mindfulness and Witchcraft: How Modern Witches Use Ancient Practices for Mental Health" by Rachel Patterson: An insightful look at how mindfulness and witchcraft intersect to support mental well-being.
- "The Role of Ritual in Mental Health" by Dr. Barbara Becker Holstein: Discusses the psychological benefits of ritual and how it can be integrated into daily life for improved mental health.

Useful Websites and Online Communities

The internet is a treasure trove of resources for those looking to learn more about witchcraft and mental health. Here are some websites and online communities that offer valuable information, support, and opportunities for connection.

Websites:

- Herb Society of America (www.herbsociety.org): Offers resources on growing, using, and sharing knowledge about herbs, including their mental health benefits.
- Mountain Rose Herbs Blog (blog.mountainroseherbs.com): Provides articles on herbal medicine, recipes, and sustainable living, with a focus on the mental and emotional benefits of herbs.
- The Herbal Academy (theherbalacademy.com): An educational resource offering online courses and articles on herbalism, including mental health applications.
- Mind Body Green (www.mindbodygreen.com): A wellness website that covers various aspects of mental health, including articles on herbal remedies, meditation, and mindfulness.

Online Communities:

- Witchvox (www.witchvox.com): A community resource network for pagans and witches, offering articles, event listings, and networking opportunities.

- Reddit - r/witchcraft: A vibrant online community where practitioners share experiences, ask questions, and offer support related to witchcraft and mental health.

- Facebook Groups: Search for groups like "Modern Witches Unite" or "Herbal Witchcraft" to find supportive communities where you can share knowledge and connect with others.

Courses and Workshops for Deeper Learning

For those looking to dive deeper into the intersection of witchcraft and mental health, there are numerous courses and workshops available. These educational opportunities provide structured learning and the chance to connect with experienced practitioners.

The Herbal Academy: Offers a range of courses from beginner to advanced levels, focusing on herbalism and its applications for health and wellness. Their courses cover topics such as creating herbal remedies, the therapeutic use of herbs, and integrating herbs into daily life.

Chestnut School of Herbal Medicine: Provides comprehensive online courses in herbal medicine, including their "Herbal Immersion Program" which delves into the medicinal and magical uses of herbs.

The School of Evolutionary Herbalism: Offers courses that blend herbal medicine with alchemical and astrological principles, providing a holistic approach to herbalism and mental health.

The Centre of Excellence: Offers a variety of courses on witchcraft, Wicca, and herbalism, including specific courses focused on mental health practices. Their "Wicca Diploma Course" and "Herbalism Diploma Course" are particularly popular.

Glastonbury Goddess Conference: An annual event held in Glastonbury, UK, featuring workshops, rituals, and presentations by leading practitioners in the fields of witchcraft, herbalism, and spiritual healing. This conference provides a unique opportunity to learn from and connect with experienced practitioners.

Local Workshops and Events: Check local metaphysical shops, community centers, and herbalist collectives for workshops and events in your area. These gatherings offer hands-on learning and the chance to meet like-minded individuals.

CHAPTER 13: CONCLUSION

Embracing Witchcraft for Mental Health

As we come to the end of this book, it's clear that witchcraft offers a rich tapestry of practices and tools that can significantly enhance mental health.

Embracing witchcraft for mental well-being involves integrating its holistic principles into your daily life, recognizing the interconnectedness of mind, body, and spirit. Through rituals, herbs, energy work, and the support of a like-minded community, you can create a balanced and empowered approach to mental health.

Witchcraft teaches us to honor the cycles of nature, to respect the energies around us, and to harness our inner power for healing and growth. By embracing these principles, you can cultivate resilience, find peace in the midst of chaos, and transform your mental and emotional landscape.

Whether you are dealing with anxiety, depression, stress, or simply seeking greater clarity and balance, the practices of witchcraft provide a path towards well-being that is both ancient and profoundly relevant to modern life.

Final Thoughts and Encouragement

As you continue on your journey, remember that the practice of witchcraft is deeply personal and ever-evolving. There is no one-size-fits-all approach, and it is essential to listen to your intuition and honor your unique path.

Be patient with yourself and allow your practices to grow and change over time. Each step you take, no matter how small, is a move towards greater self-awareness and healing.

Incorporate the rituals, techniques, and tools that resonate with you, and don't be afraid to experiment and explore new aspects of witchcraft. Keep a journal to document your experiences, insights, and progress. This will not only help you track your growth but also serve as a source of inspiration and reflection.

Surround yourself with a supportive community, whether in person or online. Sharing your journey with others who understand and appreciate your path can provide invaluable support, encouragement, and wisdom. Remember that you are not alone in this journey; the collective energy and knowledge of the witchcraft community are powerful resources to draw upon.

Above all, approach your practice with an open heart and a spirit of curiosity. Witchcraft is a beautiful and empowering path that offers endless possibilities for growth and transformation. Embrace it fully, and let it guide you towards a life of balance, peace, and profound connection.

Blessings for the Reader's Journey

As you embark on or continue your journey with witchcraft and mental health, I offer you these blessings:

May you find clarity in moments of confusion, and strength in times of challenge.

May the herbs and rituals you practice bring you healing, peace, and joy.

May your connection to the natural world deepen, grounding you and lifting your spirit.

May the light of the moon guide you, and the energy of the Earth support you.

May you always feel the presence of your community, offering you support and love.

And may you walk your path with courage, wisdom, and an open heart, embracing the magic within and around you.

Thank you for joining me on this journey through the intersection of witchcraft and mental health. May your path be filled with light, love, and endless possibilities. Blessed be.

APPENDICES

Glossary of Terms

A

Alchemy: A historical practice combining elements of chemistry, physics, astrology, art, semiotics, metallurgy, medicine, and mysticism. In herbal magic, it refers to the transformation of herbs into various forms for magical purposes.

Amulet: An object worn to protect the wearer from negative energies or to bring good luck. Often infused with specific intentions and energies.

Anointing: The application of oil, often infused with herbs, to a person or object for consecration, blessing, or protection.

Aura: An electromagnetic field that surrounds every living being, believed to reflect their physical and mental health.

B

Binding: A spell or ritual intended to restrict or contain an individual's actions or energy.

C

Cleansing: The process of removing negative energies from a person, space, or object. Methods include smudging, salt baths, and energy brushes.

Chakras: Seven main energy centers in the human body, each associated with specific physical, emotional, and spiritual functions.

Correspondences: The associations between herbs (or other items) and specific planets, elements, or deities used to enhance the effectiveness of magical work.

D

Divination: The practice of seeking knowledge of the future or the unknown through supernatural means. Methods include tarot reading, scrying, and astrology.

Deosil: Movement in a clockwise direction, often used in rituals to draw in positive energy.

E

Elixir: A medicinal potion created by infusing herbs in alcohol or water.

Energy Work: Practices that involve manipulating the body's energy fields for healing and balance, including Reiki, chakra balancing, and aura cleansing.

F

Full Moon: The phase of the moon when it is fully illuminated, often associated with completion, reflection, and celebration in rituals.

G

Grimoire: A book of magical knowledge, spells, and rituals, often passed down through generations.

Grounding: The practice of connecting oneself to the Earth to stabilize and center one's energy.

H

Herbalism: The study and use of plants for medicinal and therapeutic purposes.

I

Incense: Aromatic materials that release fragrant smoke when burned, used in rituals for cleansing, protection, and invocation.

Infusion: The process of extracting the properties of herbs by steeping them in hot water, often used in teas and medicinal preparations.

J

Journal: A personal record used to document thoughts, feelings, experiences, and progress in one's spiritual and mental health journey.

K

Knot Magic: A form of magic involving tying knots in a specific pattern to bind or release energy, intentions, or spells.

L

Lunar Phases: The different stages of the moon's cycle, each associated with specific energies and times for different types of magic and rituals.

M

Meditation: A practice involving focused attention and mindfulness to achieve a mentally clear and emotionally calm state.

Meridian Lines: Pathways in the body along which vital energy flows, used in traditional Chinese medicine and acupuncture.

N

New Moon: The phase of the moon when it is not visible from Earth, symbolizing new beginnings and setting intentions.

O

Offering: A gift given to deities, spirits, or ancestors during rituals to show respect and request assistance.

P

Pendulum: A weighted object suspended from a string or chain, used in divination to receive yes or no answers.

Planetary Hours: Specific times of the day associated with particular planets, believed to influence magical workings.

Protection Spell: A ritual performed to create a barrier of safety and repel negative energies.

Purification: The act of cleansing an object, space, or person of negative energy or impurities, often using herbs like sage or rosemary.

Q

Quartz: A versatile crystal used in various types of magic and healing, known for its amplifying properties.

R

Ritual: A set of actions performed in a prescribed order, often involving magic or spiritual practices to achieve a specific outcome.

S

Sabbat: A seasonal festival in the Wheel of the Year, celebrated by Wiccans and other pagans to mark the cycles of nature.

Sigil: A symbol created for a specific magical purpose, often imbued with personal intention and energy.

Smudging: The practice of burning herbs, typically sage, to cleanse a person, place, or object of negative energy.

Spell: A ritual performed with the intention of manifesting a specific outcome through magical means.

Solstice: The longest and shortest days of the year, marking significant points in the solar calendar celebrated in many pagan traditions.

T

Talisman: An object created with the intention of bringing good fortune, protection, or specific energies into one's life.

Tarot: A deck of cards used in divination to gain insights and guidance about the past, present, and future.

U

Umbra: The fully shaded inner region of a shadow cast by an opaque object, often used metaphorically in rituals dealing with the subconscious or hidden aspects.

V

Visualization: The practice of using mental imagery to achieve specific outcomes or enhance meditation and magical work.

W

Waning Moon: The phase of the moon when it is decreasing in size, associated with introspection, release, and rest.

Wicca: A modern pagan, witchcraft religion that emphasizes the worship of nature and the practice of magic.

Y

Yule: The pagan festival celebrating the winter solstice, marking the return of longer days and the rebirth of the sun.

Z

Zenith: The highest point in the sky reached by a celestial body, often used in astrology and magic to signify the peak of energy or power.

Quick Reference Guides for Herbal Properties

- Chamomile (Matricaria chamomilla):
  - Properties: Calm, peace, healing
  - Uses: Teas for relaxation, baths for soothing skin, sachets for promoting sleep
- Lavender (Lavandula angustifolia):
  - Properties: Relaxation, love, protection
  - Uses: Essential oils for calming, teas for anxiety, sachets for restful sleep
- Peppermint (Mentha × piperita):
  - Properties: Clarity, energy, purification
  - Uses: Teas for digestive aid, essential oils for focus, sprays for refreshing the aura
- Rosemary (Rosmarinus officinalis):
  - Properties: Memory, protection, purification
  - Uses: Teas for memory enhancement, smudging for purification, oils for focus
- Ginger (Zingiber officinale):
  - Properties: Strength, success, energy
  - Uses: Teas for digestive health, tinctures for energy, essential oils for invigorating the mind

- Echinacea (Echinacea purpurea):
    - Properties: Immunity, healing, protection
    - Uses: Teas and tinctures for immune support, salves for skin healing
- Calendula (Calendula officinalis):
    - Properties: Healing, clarity, protection
    - Uses: Salves for skin issues, teas for internal healing, baths for soothing and protection
- Rose (Rosa spp.):
    - Properties: Love, beauty, harmony
    - Uses: Teas for love, baths for relaxation, essential oils for beauty rituals
- Sage (Salvia officinalis):
    - Properties: Purification, protection, wisdom
    - Uses: Smudging for cleansing, teas for wisdom, oils for protection
- Yarrow (Achillea millefolium):
    - Properties: Healing, protection, courage
    - Uses: Teas for internal healing, salves for wounds, smudging for protection

Planetary Correspondences:

- Sun: Vitality, success, protection
  Herbs: Sunflower, St. John's Wort, Chamomile

- Moon: Intuition, dreams, emotional healing
  Herbs: Mugwort, Jasmine, Sandalwood

- Mercury: Communication, intellect, travel
  Herbs: Lavender, Dill, Peppermint

- Venus: Love, beauty, harmony
  Herbs: Rose, Thyme, Yarrow

- Mars: Strength, courage, protection
  Herbs: Basil, Garlic, Nettle

- Jupiter: Growth, prosperity, luck
  Herbs: Sage, Oak, Mint

- Saturn: Banishing, grounding, protection
  Herbs: Cypress, Myrrh, Comfrey

Elemental Correspondences:

- Earth: Grounding, stability, prosperity
  Herbs: Patchouli, Vetiver, Comfrey

- Air: Intellect, communication, freedom
  Herbs: Lavender, Dill, Lemongrass

- Fire: Passion, transformation, protection
  Herbs: Basil, Cinnamon, Garlic

- Water: Healing, love, intuition
  Herbs: Chamomile, Rose, Lemon Balm

Astrological Correspondences:

- Aries: Basil, Nettle, Ginger
- Taurus: Rose, Sage, Thyme
- Gemini: Lavender, Dill, Peppermint
- Cancer: Mugwort, Jasmine, Lemon Balm
- Leo: Sunflower, St. John's Wort, Chamomile
- Virgo: Rosemary, Lavender, Caraway
- Libra: Rose, Thyme, Yarrow
- Scorpio: Basil, Garlic, Nettle
- Sagittarius: Sage, Oak, Mint
- Capricorn: Cypress, Myrrh, Comfrey
- Aquarius: Lavender, Lemongrass, Rosemary
- Pisces: Chamomile, Rose, Lemon Balm

These quick reference guides provide a handy overview of the properties and correspondences of various herbs, helping you integrate them into your magical and mental health practices effectively.

Further Reading from the Modern Witchcraft & Wicca series by Mark Hutchinson

Available Now on Amazon.com

Modern Witchcraft & Wicca - The Enchanted Path

The Art of Divination

Elemental Magic: Earth, Fire, AIr & Water

Advanced Spellcasting Guide

The Green Witch's Encyclopedia: Herbs, Magic & Healing

Witchcraft & Mental Health in the 21st Century

If you have found value in these books please help us reach a larger audience by leaving a review on Amazon or Google. It really does help small publishers in a big way. Thank you.

Hutchinson Publishing

www.ingramcontent.com/pod-product-compliance
Lightning Source LLC
Chambersburg PA
CBHW061056250726
48653CB00001B/429

9798332760068